HOW TO PATENT

Practical Steps To Patent, Copyright, And Trademark For All, Including BONUS Amazon And Private Label

Bradley James

DISCLAIMER

All knowledge contained in this book is given for informational and educational purposes only. The author is not accountable for any results or outcomes that emanate from using this material. Constructive attempts have been made to provide both accurate and effective information, but the author is not bound for the accuracy or use/misuse of this information.

INTRODUCTION

In Developing countries, one thing that is easily ignored is Intellectual Property Protection. Even in developed countries where the culture of IP (Intellectual Property) protection culture is established, it has been treated more like an "on-paper" right rather than something that binds the public from infringing on the works of creators and inventors.

There are so many creators globally, and it is even believed that the greatest inventions are yet to happen. If this is the case, it is only important that creators are enlightened about the process of IP protection.

This book sheds light on all the terms and processes involved in Intellectual Protection in the most relatable ways possible. It uses everyday terms and situations to enlighten readers in layman's terms. The reason for this is not far-fetched. There are so many complexities associated with IP Protection and its processes that people are scared even to educate themselves about it because it may be a fruitless effort. Therefore, it is not surprising that they leave all the work to IP Protection lawyers and keep themselves in the dark.

With this book, you could possess far more exhaustive knowledge of Intellectual Property Protection than most experts. This is not an exaggerated attempt to get you to read it, but if you turn over the pages, you will get so much information about IP Protection that even the internet does not offer. There is everything about patents, Copyright, and Trademarks. The book enlightens you on how to apply these forms of IP Protection. It also describes why it is imperative for everyone who owns a work of art or an invention to protect their creation in very objective ways.

Hence, ***Practical Steps to Patent, Copyright, and Trademark for All, Including Amazon and Libel,*** is not like any other book about Intellectual property. Instead, it offers far more than expected. But how would you know unless you turn over the pages? Well, shall we begin?

CHAPTER ONE
Understanding Patent, Copyright, and Trademark

Many people generally assume that Patents, Copyright, and Trademark all fall under the same category and probably mean the same thing. While it may be true that they all fall under the category of certification, they mean something different entirely. This is because their definitions show so many differences. For a layman, their differences in definitions might be the singular technical word that each term possesses. However, in this case, it is not so. This chapter will expound on the differences between Patents, Copyright, and Trademark in the most relatable ways possible.

Meanwhile, this chapter aims not only to show you the differences between these seemingly technical terms but also to enlighten you so much on each of the terms that you can easily pick out the differences between them without the help of an expert. Ready? Let's get into it!

Patent

Before we get into a textbook explanation of a Patent, let us examine its definition in an everyday situation. Let's say you come up with an idea; for example, you come up with an idea for how to make a machine and write down your thoughts as you think them (Sounds impossible? well, it's an example). Now, not only did you come up with this idea, but you also found some ways to implement its actuality. You might have discussed this innovation

with your friends or a colleague, and they might have even offered insights on more steps to actualizing your innovation.
As humans, it is only normal that we share our innovations with people, especially when they are so out-of-the-box. But meanwhile, you need to be careful because someone might try to steal that innovation as theirs, and there is no way you would prove that the idea was originally yours. So what do you do?
A patent is a certification that gives you legal and exclusive rights to an idea, innovation, or intellectual property, especially if the property offers something new. A patent is more like "an idea protector" in which no one would be able to steal your idea, sell it, or claim it as theirs because you now have the exclusive right over it. In this case, the idea of a machine that can write down your thoughts as you think them can very much be patented because it is what no one has done before, and you want to do it. Government Agencies usually grant a Patent after the application to Patent an Idea or intellectual property is made to them.
It is important to note that Patents are not just idea stampers as many people would think. It doesn't imply that you think of something and walk down to the Agency responsible for Patenting to get your idea stamped as yours. It is not as simple as that. Certain procedures accompany getting an idea patented. Although the procedures for patenting an idea or intellectual property differ from country to country, some similarities can be singled out in these procedures. Here are a few things that are usually required in a Patent procedure.

Claims

Claims in a Patenting process involve spelling out the ideas or intellectual property that the patent is to protect. The subject matter of the intellectual property is spelled out as comprehensively as possible to enhance clarification. This is to make sure that the entire process and idea and the intellectual property are written out in clear terms. Anyone who comes with a similar idea or process would not be given the right over it because it's already yours. For example, for our "impossible" mind-reader

machine, a claim for it could read:
"A Machine for reading people's minds and writing it down on a piece of paper"
Of course, this is only the theme of the claim. Other details like the equipment that will make up the machine and how the machine is to be made will be included in the claim.

Novelty

This is another word for originality. You can't patent an idea that has been in existence or what is already known to everyone. Patenting does not work that way. For example, you can't patent an idea to develop a chemical that kills mosquitoes. It doesn't matter if the chemical kills mosquitoes faster and can kill the mosquitoes in the whole world; what matters is that it is not an original idea. In Patent, Novelty is a necessary procedure because it aims to prevent an idea or intellectual property that has been patented before from being patented again. There will be a clash of legal rights over the intellectual property in question in this case. Novelty prevents that from happening.

INVENTIVENESS/ NON-OBVIOUSNESS

For intellectual property to be patented, it has to be non-obvious. For example, we all know that Johannes Gutenberg is credited for designing and building the first printing press. Meanwhile, if someone comes up with an idea for a printing press that automatically prints out colored papers rather than the white ones, such an idea would not be patented because it is too obvious. Here is how non-obviousness works under patenting: If the idea to be patented is similar to an idea that already exists and follows the production or development of that idea, such an idea would not be patented because it is uninventive. It is not a new invention but a variation of what has been invented before. It's like how someone develops a manual blender and gets credit for it. If someone else were to think of making an electric blender, such a person would not get credit for it because it is a variation of an already established and known invention.

Usefulness

Let's be realistic; what is the essence of an idea or intellectual property that sounds so smart but is no real use to anyone? For example, if someone comes up with an idea of attracting b butterflies to a particular place and making them stay as long as forever, such an idea cannot be patented. The reason is not far-fetched. It sounds interesting, but it's not of real use to anyone. In the case of a patent, the plan is to register the most useful innovations to mankind and give credit to whoever came up with such innovation. Hence patent does not involve having a novel idea alone; it involves having a novel idea useful to everyone. Out of all the requirements needed to get an intellectual property patented, it would seem that usefulness is the most important and compulsory one.

Copyright

As earlier implied, Copyright and Patent fall under the same category. However, while a Patent gives the exclusive legal right to a new invention, a Copyright is used to provide exclusive legal rights to creators or authors on works of art such as music, films, advertisement, books, paintings, technical drawings, maps, etc. So you see, while a Patent focuses on only giving the exclusive legal right to a new curated idea or invention, copyright recognizes the re-creation of art by a particular person. This is why you can't get a book patented, but you can get a copyright on it. It is also why you can't get a copyright for an invention, but you can get it patented.
Copyright establishes that while creating a particular art is not the first of its kind, it still needs to be protected to prevent intellectual theft. Copyright recognizes a creator or author's right to intellectual property like Patents. This right granted by copyright allows the author to replicate or copy several of their works of art and sell or distribute them to members of the public. This right makes them the only ones that can do something like that. For this reason, it becomes an illegal act for anyone to sell or replicate a work of art that has been copyrighted. Such a person could go to jail. People who pirate movies and music fall under this category.
Although copyright has its standard procedures, its procedures are not as complex or lengthy as Patents. The major requirement for Copyright is Originality. The work of art must be the sole idea of the author and must not be related to any other person's creation. While patent focuses on uniqueness, copyright focuses on originality. Copyright is not concerned with whether or not a work of art is the first of its kind; it focuses on whether or not that kind of art has been made before". This is why someone else can't publish a book titled "Pride and Prejudice."

Meanwhile, there have been some cases where some books had the same titles. This is possible. As inferred, the point of copyright is originality, not uniqueness. If the books have the same title, then the ideas or storyline must be completely different. For example, in 2018, after the publication of Tomi Adeyemi's popular Young-Adult fantasy novel titled "Children of Blood and Bone," another author- Nora Roberts- published her novel titled "Of Blood and Bone." Although Tomi Adeyemi did not find this satisfactory, Nora Roberts confirmed that the ideas and storylines in the books were completely different, and she had not even heard of Tomi Adeyemi's book before.
Likewise, in the case of music, many songs can have the same titles, but of course, the song themes, lyrics, and sounds have to be different. We all know John Legend owns "All of me," but there can be another song titled "All of me." However, this does not mean copyright is not being as protective of art as possible. If anything, copyright is very specific when it comes to art protection. If an artist samples the sound of another artist or sound, credit has to be given to such Artist. The artists can decide that they don't want to have their sounds sampled on another work of art, and the Artist that wants to sample that sound will not do so again because they don't have the right to it. For example, when Beyoncé made The Lion King album, she sampled some sounds from a Nigerian Artist after permission was given, and credit had to be given to that Nigerian Artist. That is how protective art Copyright can be.

Trademark

Like Patents and Copyrights, a trademark aims to protect intellectual property or art; the only major difference is that a Trademark is a sign that distinguishes an art or goods and services of a company from another one that is similarly related to it. In other words, a trademark allows for recognizing a specific product as belonging to a particular company or person. Trademark does not protect products or services alone; it is also used to distinguish a brand or company from another. For

example, Facebook can't use Twitter's same bird logo. Twitter already trademarked that Logo, and Facebook, or any company whatsoever, cannot use that logo.
As its name implies, a trademark marks the name of products or brands. This is usually the signs ©, ®, ™; where:
®- Represents "Registered."
©- Represents "Copyright."
™- Represents "Trademarked."

The Importance of Protecting Intellectual Property
(Patent, Copyright, Trademark)

Whether Trademarks, Copyright, or Patent, it is very important that intellectual property is protected. Although the reasons for this have been inferred in discussions made above in the previous sections, it is only necessary that these reasons are singled out for greater understanding.

Theft

This can never be overemphasized. We live in a world where people would love to profit from other people's lifework or creation unapologetically. It is even surprising that even though creators protect their music and movies, it still gets exposed to illegal streaming platforms and downloads. Once you get your (IP) Intellectual Property protected, you have the legal right to file a lawsuit against anyone who attempts to pirate your work. Not only will you win the case, but you will also win millions of money from such a person or brand, depending on the amount of damage made.
IP Protection is like insurance; in fact, it is insurance. It ensures your intellectual property against those who will replicate or copy it.

Promotion of Innovations and Inventions

One major purpose of IP Protection is that it helps to promote more innovations and inventions among creators. Let us assume there is no IP Protection like Patent, Trademark, or

Copyright; inventors would have their works replicated as many times. They would not reap the benefits of their labor or creation. The recognition for their work may get lost, and everyone may start claiming ownership of it. For example, if Johannes Guttenberg did not lay claims to the Printing Press and patented it, we might not have known who invented such art, and credit would not be given to Johannes for his brilliant masterpiece.
The work of creators and artists must get protected to encourage other inventors and creators to develop brilliant ideas and get rewarded for their work.

Value

When Intellectual property is protected, there is an indication that a form of value has been stamped on such intellectual property. Once people realize that you have protected your intellectual property, it increases the value of such property. The indirect result of this is the commercial success of your creation. For example, let's say you have a business trademark your logo; this shows people that you own exclusive legal rights to that brand and its products and services. With the commercial success of your brand or creation, you can raise a lot of money to create such art further.

Challenges of Protecting Intellectual Property

The major challenge of IP Protection has been **infringement**. Over the years, especially in all countries worldwide, infringement on intellectual property has become rampant. There have been several illegal downloads of music, movies, and art. We all know there is only one Mona Lisa in the world, but there have been so many Mona Lisa paintings after Leonardo's own. The fact that most of those who infringe on the legal right of creators get away with it is a great challenge for creators and IP Protection in general. There are so many sites that promote illegal downloads, and these sites have not been taken down or charged. Most of these sites have been in existence for years, making millions of money off another person's lifework.

It is even harder for software developers to track the recognition of their creations because of the complexities that accompany the certifications of these creations. In addition, the complexities involved in Intellectual Property law have made it difficult for creators to establish their exclusive rights to their works.

Understanding the difference between Asset and Right

It is easy to confuse both terms, especially regarding IP Protection. An asset refers to a resource (goods, services, capital) that can serve as an economic benefit for an individual, organization, or government. Such an asset can generate continuous cash flow for the owner. On the other hand, right is the exclusive recognition of a person's access to an asset or intellectual property.

Key Takeaways from this chapter:

- IP Protection is insurance for ownership recognition and against theft or infringement.
- While Patent trademarks and Copyright fall under the same category of IP Protection, they are used to protect different forms of creations.
- Patents recognize the exclusive rights of a creator based on innovation. At the same time, copyright acknowledges the right of an author based on the re-creation of art by a particular person. Trademark establishes the symbol for a business, brand, or product.
- The emphasis of Patents is on novelty, inventiveness, and usefulness. For copyright, the emphasis is on originality, while trademark emphasizes distinguishing ownership.

CHAPTER TWO

Creating and Owning my Patent

The first chapter of this book has enlightened you exhaustively about Patents, Copyright, and Trademarks. This was important to make it easier for you to grasp the vocabulary of Patents, Copyright, and Trademarks that will be used throughout this book. It will also make understanding the processes involved in protecting Intellectual Properties relatively easy.
Creating your patent may seem like a complex process, but once you have all the required things needed to have a Patent, it becomes just like another registration.

How to Create and Own a Patent

The Qualification Process

Chapter One clearly stated that the emphasis of getting a Patent is on Usefulness, Novelty, and Inventiveness. This is referred to as the qualification process. If you do not have these, you cannot create or own a patent. Once you have all these, you have ticked most of the boxes and are ready to get a Patent of your own. Here are the processes involved with getting a Patent.

Get an Attorney

First, it should be noted that several creators and inventors have created and owned a patent without the services of an attorney. These inventors had no problems in the process of creating their Patents. If you live in the United States, the law mandates examiners at the US Patent and Trademark Office to help inventors who have no lawyer. This further helps the

inventors because the assumption is that most inventors may not know enough about Intellectual Property compared to people who are experts in the field.
However, you should get an attorney. Do not get just an Attorney; get an attorney specializing in IP (Intellectual Property) Law. Apart from the fact that such an Attorney will work you through every single detail of the process of creating your patent, the attorney is bound to make your patent creation faster compared to officials who have been mandated to do so at the USPTO (US Patent and Trademark Office).
Besides, one of the most delicate things about ownership is when it comes to Intellectual Property. There is always a thousand in a million chance that a mistake can be made which will negatively impact any Patent you create and own consequently. For example, many music artists sign contracts to record labels that take control of their intellectual property even when they leave the label. Sometimes, they even lose their stage name and certain things that further wrecks their music career. It is not so different with IP.
Also, when you want to get an IP Lawyer, make sure it is someone that comes highly recommended and has been in practice for a long time. Getting a Rookie IP Lawyer is almost no different from getting no IP Lawyer.

Record your claims (The Specification Process)

If you remember vividly, Chapter one discussed what claims are in a patenting process. Claims involve spelling out the ideas or intellectual property that the patent is to protect. While inventing your idea, you must have recorded the steps involved in the invention. At this stage, you must leave nothing out. If you didn't record everything during the invention process, you should deliberately set time out to do all that in a book. This is highly imperative because patenting an Intellectual property such as innovation requires specific details. Every diagram must be accounted for. This may sound a little dramatic, but it doesn't hurt to have these things written out comprehensively. The USPTO requires that you include:

- The title of your invention
- A thorough background of your invention
- An exhaustive summary of the process of the invention

Advisably, and more importantly, you should already have a prototype of your invention. This makes it easier because it allows the patenting office to see and test how your invention works, which further clarifies the process. In addition, when you are done with keeping a record of your claims and the invention process, you must have two reliable witnesses sign your record to confirm that what you are building has been for a time and is wholly your property.

Financials

Yes, let's talk financials. There are financial implications for applying for a Patent, and you need to be sure that your invention can compensate you for any amount of money spent while acquiring a patent. Indeed, you may not need to pay more than a few thousand dollars while applying for a patent, but you may need to pay attention to more than that if you want your patent to have some use if you finally get it.

Usually, inventors are recommended to have investors who are very much willing to back up a technological invention after it is patented. This is because patents expire. The expiry date of patents varies from country to country, but in the United States, patents don't expire until twenty years. That may seem like many years, but you must have enough profit returns from your invention because once twenty years are up, you cannot renew the patent again. It goes directly into the public domain.

Meanwhile, some countries allow for Patent Renewal- if you are in India, but for the United States, there is no Patent renewal; once a patent expires, individual ownership of it is no longer recognized. This is why enough investments must be made before getting a Patent to make the most out of it within the twenty years that you own the rights to it. Patents cannot be renewed in countries like the US because someone can want to improve existing technologies, and long-lasting patents will hinder this. Hence, there is no renewal of patents in the United States, so it doesn't kill the innovation of others and disrupts inventions and development.

Once you get the financials for your invention set up, you can start paying attention to the next important thing- which is conducting a Patent search.

Conducting a Patent Search/Novelty Search

The importance of this stage cannot be overemphasized. First, you have to make sure your invention is new. This is so your application to create a patent is not denied. To do this, you must conduct an intensive Patent search. The essence of this is to find erstwhile inventions similar to yours.

First, you need to search the US Patents inventory to see if there are similar inventions to yours. If you are done with this, it is important to search the patent inventories of other foreign countries. These inventories may not be as wholesome as possible to show every single patent that has been created with inventions similar to yours. What you need to do is search journals and publications. Also, you may want to check the internet and search the Patent and Trademark Depository Library. Then, visit the USPTO (US Patent and Trademark Office) website. It is free for you to conduct your patent search. Also, you should use Google Patent Website- which is also free. Their patent records dating back to the 17th century! If you want your patent search to be more exhaustive, you may use the services of companies that offer patent search for a small fee. These companies include Sagacious IP, PatBase, Clarivate, and Cardinal Intellectual Property.

Show the Difference

To be honest, the chance that there has not been an invention similar to yours in making, idea, or style is ten out of a million. However, this doesn't mean you still can't get a patent.

You just have to show how very different your technology is compared to theirs. This may sound confusing to you since one of the major requirements for getting a Patent is a novelty.
Here is how it works: Let's say someone already invented cars, and now you want to invent electric cars. Both forms are means of transportation and are cars. However, your invention can be patented because it has better and improved technology. The only way your patents cannot be created is if you were to create another car brand. That way, what you need to create is a trademark, not a patent.

File an Application with the US Patent and Trademark Office

When you are done with the steps mentioned above, you are ready to apply. At this stage, there are two types of Patents you can file; one is optional, and the other is required. The optional one is called "Provisional Patent Application" (PPA), while the required one is called "Regular Patent Application."
As the name implies, a Provisional Patent Application (PPA) is given temporarily. It is used to indicate your claim on a patent currently pending status. This is usually not costly at all. For example, in the United States, Small companies pay an approximate \$150 while large companies pay an approximate \$300. However, you must file an RPA within a year of filing a PPA so that you don't lose your claim of the Provisional Patent Application.
Also, you can decide to file for a Regular Patent Application straightaway (RPA). This involves all the necessary processes, and a permanent patent is created for you once you file an RPA. It is recommended that inventors and creators file a PPA application first to lay claim to a patent.
When all this is done, you can then proceed to file your Patent application electronically through the USPTO electronic filing system or the mail.

Creating and Owning my Copyright

The inarguable truth is that the moment you create

something, you automatically own the copyright to that thing. However, in the case of ownership disputes, you are legally required to create and own copyright so that the government and the public recognize your right to that creation. Creating a copyright of your own is relatively easy compared to creating and owning a Patent. All you need to do is visit your country's Copyright Office through their traditional office or website. You need to provide proof of your work to them by sending them a copy of what you have created or a link to it- in the case that it is something like music or a movie- which can easily be pirated. Electronic filing is often said to be faster than the traditional method. However, this may still take up to five months, depending on your country.

Creating and Owning my Trademark

Like Patenting, creating and owning a trademark is almost always done by the government body charged with patenting, and the process is always the same, too- except that it is way less tricky than that of patents. Creating and owning a trademark is also done by the USPTO in the US. Meanwhile, like patenting, it also takes more time. It doesn't matter if you haven't set up your company or brand yet. You must get a trademark before you set up your brand to confirm that your brand or company has not been in use by someone else.

Here are the processes involved in creating and owning a patent.

Conduct a Research

You have to be sure no brand or company uses the logo or the name you intend to use. This may be tricky- considering that there are millions of companies in the world. However, your search can be made easy when you check the Trademark depository of different countries. You can assess the US Trademark Electronic Search System and go through previous trademarks that have been created. This does not mean you should not search for names related to your brand too. For example, Jackson Vile Foods and Jackson Ville Foods (Double "L) sound too similar. Your trademark can be denied because of similarity.

Apply for your Trademark

The next step is applying for your trademark. You can do this online on the USPTO website or through the USPTO itself. There are usually ten parts to the application:

- Your name and address
- The country you were born in or the country you have citizenship of
- A diagram/drawing that shows your brand logo as well as the name of your brand or company
- The name you want to be recognized with the brand for future correspondences
- A concise description of what your brand does
- Your signature or that of your representative (Preferably and advisably; your signature)
- The class of the goods and services your brand is to provide
- A description of these goods (products) or services
- A fee to be paid for the application
- The date the brand will be in use or the date it has been in use.

Filing your Trademark application

Once you are done filling out your application, all left is to apply. There are usually two options available for filing a trademark. There is the TEAS Plus filing option and the TEAS standard filing option. For the TEAS Plus filing option, the fee paid is low. It is usually $250. Meanwhile, it has more requirements than the TEAS Standard Filing Option. But it has a positive side; it has a very low rate of rejections.

On the other hand, The TEAS Standard filing option is more expensive in comparison. But it has fewer requirements and is easier to process. The fee is usually $350. You should use the TEAS Standard filing option when you don't have all the information required to feel all the compulsory fields in the TEAS Plus Filing option.

As soon as you have submitted your application for a Trademark consideration, you will get a receipt from the USPTO confirming that you have applied and paid. You will also be given a serial number. With this serial number, you can visit (TSDR) The Trademark Status and Document Retrieval Portal to check if your Trademark application has been approved or not.

Maintaining Confidentiality with your Ideas

The delicateness of something as significant as intellectual property begs the responsibility to maintain confidentiality with it no matter the circumstance. But one question is left hanging in the air; how do you maintain confidentiality with your ideas if you need more hands to help you actualize them?

This is indeed a reasonable question, and if you have been asking it, you are smart and realistic. However, the truth is that there are many instances where we come up with an idea or an innovation or create something, and we know that it is just impossible for us to achieve that thing alone unless we involve others. The reason for this is not far-fetched.

Let's say you want to make a technological or scientific invention, and you know a lot about science or technology (as the case may be), you already have the formula or the processes all laid up, but you need someone or a group of professionals to piece it all together. However, you don't, and in fact, should not trust people to keep the processes to themselves or try to replicate what you are doing. Therefore, here are a few steps to help you maintain confidentiality with your ideas.

Make the system work for you.

We always underestimate the power of a legal contract. It is even funny that we allow ourselves to feel so secure that we believe that people who are close to us and are working with us on these ideas can never steal our ideas. It is nothing personal, but businesses don't always thrive on assumptions and taking the trust of close people for granted. If you are working on a creative process- whether inventing a new technology or making an album or a movie- have the people involved sign an NDA (Non-disclosure Agreement) and an agreement that prevents them from stealing or replicating your work. Also, have them sign an agreement that they just first heard of the work to be created when you employed them so that they don't say they've had the idea before. All this you can do in a simple legal document. Of course, you must have an attorney (preferably an IP Lawyer).

It sounds like a lot of work, but better be safe than be stolen from.

Discipline

This may sound motivational, but it is the truth. You need to tell yourself that you will not share your idea or creation with people until it has been certified that it is legally yours. Understandably, we get excited about an idea, and we can't wait to tell our friends and family about it. Sometimes, it is impossible not to share these things with our families or those close to us, but it is recommended that the explicit details should not be shared with them. All it takes is one person telling another person, and then the idea becomes public, and someone else might claim it.

The amusing thing about patents is that if someone were part of your process and didn't put them under any contract, they could steal your work and file a patent before you do, thereby making them the rightful owner of the work. But, of course, it would be hard to dispute this, and the case would go to court. So you have to make sure that you are giving less anytime someone brings your invention or work of creation up as a subject.

Key Takeaways from this chapter

- To Create and own a patent, you have to record all the processes of your invention or creation.
- Afterward, you need to conduct a patent search to find out inventions that are similar to yours
- Automatically, you own the copyright to something once you create it, but you should get government copyright in the case of ownership disputes and certifications for future purposes.
- To create and own a Patent and or a Trademark, you need to apply and file with the USPTO (If you live in the United States).
- You must maintain confidentiality with your intellectual property. This can best be done through legally binding contracts such as NDAs.

CHAPTER 3

Claims: An Extensive Guide

Without gainsaying, it is evident you know what claims are now. Simply, claims to highlight the subject matter of an invention during the process of a patent application. The only way to know if an invention is real or if it was infringed upon is through claims. Sometimes, claims are expressed in such legal and technical terms that it may require an IP lawyer's help to outline the necessary details of the claims of an invention during patent application. It is usually recommended (if not compulsory) that inventors or creators have a prototype of their inventions. This is because it becomes easy for the Patent office to see the things explained in the claims through the prototype. This is simple; you cannot lay claims to things that your invention cannot do. If a claim is meant to protect your invention for what it can do, then it definitely cannot protect your invention for what it cannot do. In the next sections of this chapter, there will be a description of the categories of claims and their major types.

Staking your Claims

Staking Claims refers to all the processes involved in securing your Intellectual Property. This case explains how it is important for you to make the most out of the various claims available to ensure that your claims on a product or process are protected fully. This is why there are different types of claims. Therefore, when you are told to "Stake your claim," you should secure your IP with as many tight claims as you can. This brings us to the various types of claims we have and the ones you should consider while staking your claims.

Types/Categories of Claims

Some articles or publications recognize only two types of Claims. Some recognize four, while others say there are more than four. Based on this, this section has compiled the list of claims to make you examine these claims about their role in staking your claims.

Product Claims

Product Claims are called so because they refer to claims made on an invention that is a physical entity. It is a claim that involves physical products like devices, machines, and/or a computer program. With this kind of claim, there is a vivid description of the elements that make up the product.

Process/Method Claim

This is the direct opposite of the product claims. Process claims are also called "Method Claims," The reason for this is that they are used to list out the steps involved in making an invention. It is simply referred to as claims to an activity. Process claims are used when the invention in question is based on activity than the product itself. For example, if someone discovered a serum that cures HIV. The patent claims will be a process because the emphasis is on the activity involved during the making of that serum- in this case, the activity done by the creator in a medical laboratory.

The gerund verb "-ing" is always common in-process claims because it has to do with a broad but concise description of how the invention was made. How these claims are written depends on the field. This is based on the realization that inventions are not limited to the technological field alone. There are constant inventions in the medical field too, and the vocabulary employed during process claims has to be functional and sound professional. This means it must not be written in a personal or relatable way. It has to be formal and descriptive enough about the field.

Product-by-Process Claims

You must have certainly heard of a form of claim called the "Product-by-Process Claims." This was invented by the United States when it seemed that claims description of inventions during the patent application process was not exhaustive enough. Simply, a product-by-process claim is used to claim a product defined by the process used to make it. This form of claim is the combination of both product and process claims. But the specification of the product involved may necessarily require this form of claim to be used. Although this form of claim was rejected some time based on its Indefiniteness, it has now become acceptable in the US. This is because some inventions are products and cannot be well protected unless the Product-by-Process claims method is applied.

For example, if there were a cream that could cure a certain type of skin cancer, such cream would be patented, but the best way to patent such a cream is through a product-by-process claim. This is because another person or brand can duplicate the processes involved in making the cream, and such infringement would not be illegal. After all, the process itself has not been protected under patent claims.

These categories of claims can all be used during patent applications. However, one can only choose to use the product claim, the process claim, or the product-by-Process claim. However, they cannot be used arbitrarily unless the product in question necessitates it.

Composition Claim

A composition claim is used if the invention process involves a chemical procedure, i.e., chemicals are involved during the making of the invention. Usually, this is classified under process claims, but it has been realized that not all process claims have chemical components in them. Many process claims do not usually involve chemicals. Hence, a composition claim is necessary so that the elements used to make the invention will be protected.

Apparatus Claim

An apparatus claim gives a vivid description of the network of systems present in a machine or device. This is necessary to outline every single component present in the invention. An Apparatus claim is usually used for a product invention.

Mean Plus Function Claim

The Mean Plus Function Claim is also used to protect product inventions. As its name implies, it refers to the functionality of the components of an invention. Therefore, it is not concerned about the structure or feature of the invention but rather with its functionality.

Dependent and Independent Claim

These are the most common types of claims under patenting. An independent claim is a standalone claim that explains or describes the features of a claim, while a Dependent Claim elaborates on these features. Hence, a dependent claim refers to an independent claim and includes the features present in an independent claim. A claim can contain more than one independent and dependent claim.

Beauregard Claim

This type of claim is specifically to protect software inventions and any other kind of inventions related to software. The emphasis on this type of patent claim is whether or not the software works and works well. Although the claim also includes the composition of the claim, this is just a formality and not the focus of the Beauregard Claim.

Jepson Claim

Jepson's claims are usually improvement claims. They describe how new technology improves on old technology and maintain that the new technology still retains an amount of novelty- which is one of the requirements for getting a Patent.

However, this patent does not have worldwide recognition but is primarily used in the US.

Checking Previous Claims

Before you make claims on an invention, you must check previous claims to ensure that your claims are not synonymous with those made before. This could lead to your application getting denied. Similar claims only scream one thing- that you might want to infringe on the invention of another person- which may not be so. But that is the whole point of it. Claims are meant to protect the features and composition of an invention from getting infringed upon by another person. This is why you must check the previous claims made.

You don't need to carry out an extensive search on this. All you need to do is check previous claims that have similarities with your inventions if you find related or similar claims. You can use the Jepson claims to show how invention improves on an old one and still maintains its novelty. This is one of the advantages of having several types of claims.

Key Takeaways from this Chapter

- It is important to stake your claims after you are sure you own intellectual property. Staking your claims has to do with the different combinations of claims you use in your patent application to secure your IP
- Before staking your claims, you must check previous claims and see how they are similar to yours. This will help shape your claims appropriately and ensure that your patent application does not get denied.
- There are ten types of claims mentioned in this chapter (With the separation of dependent and independent claims). The essence of these many claims is to find the best possible ways for inventors to stake their claims on their IP.
- Also, these various kinds of claims help to protect all kinds of inventions based on their field and specification.

CHAPTER 4
Patents and their Types

The Previous chapter of this book talked about applying for a Patent. However, as elaborate as the explanations are, they still have not covered some more steps required to apply for a Patent. Patent Application goes more than just filling out a form online or sending it through the mail; the many steps involved are crucial and need to be followed. In light of this, this chapter will explain a few more things you need to learn during applying for a patent. First, there will be an insight into the types of patent applications.

Types of Patents

There are three types of Patents. These patents may not be recognized worldwide but have significant recognition in the United States. They are Utility, Plant, and Design Patent.

Utility Patent

In most countries globally, Utility Patent is widely recognized and used. It is also a common form of patent. A Utility Patent is the patent given to an invention borne out of pure novelty and inventiveness. This patent can be obtained for a machine that offers a new method of doing things differently. It could also be for a process or a composition.

In other words, the point of a Utility patent is uniqueness. It is the kind of patent granted to completely inventive discoveries that show a new of doing things that have been done before. Because it is the model kind of patent that has all the characteristics of what a Patent should be, a Utility patent can have several claims to protect it. As the name implies, this invention is of great use, and

its function in society cannot be trumped.
There are many documents used for the application of a utility patent, and the most important of these documents are:

- A Transmittal Application sheet specifically for the Utility patent
- A fee determination Record Form
- Power of Attorney
- Information Disclosure Statement
- Filing Fees
- Recordation Form Cover Sheet
- A fee transmittal for the fiscal year
- A Declaration of mailing
- Evidence of Confirmation of Receipt

Summarily, a Utility Patent is filed to get optimum protection for an invention and its functionality.

Design Patent
While Utility Patent is filed for a novel invention and protects the functionality of such invention, Design Patent is the kind of patent that protects the design of the invention; this protection covers the look of the invention, so it doesn't get parodied or replicated by other people. The essence of a Design Patent is to make sure that novel inventions get the possible protection as possible against infringement. It doesn't matter if the utility of an invention is protected because it is useful; if the design is not protected through patents, it can be used by other people or brands, and they may not face legal consequences because it doesn't belong to them- technically. However, if the utility and design of an invention are patented, it is as protected as possible. Examples of Design patents include designs on jewelry, automobiles, or designs on any product.
Therefore, the point is that while the usefulness of an invention should be protected, the visual qualities and the beauty of the design should be protected as well, especially if this design has

unique features. Meanwhile, unlike the Utility patent, a design patent only lasts 14-15 years- at least in the United States. It may last longer than this in other countries.

Plant Patent

This is the rarest of patents because plants do not get patented often. These plants have to be natural, somatic or bred if they do. Not only these, but they also have to be discovered or invented. The delicateness of discovering or inventing a plant has placed so many requirements on getting a plant patented.

First, what are the odds that all the plants in the world have not been discovered? Let us entertain the presumption and assume that there is a chance that all the plants in the world have not been discovered. However, walking or exploring in a forest, and finding a new plant that no one knows or has seen before, does not count as a discovery. It already exists naturally.

You may seem surprised since it is stated above that the law covers the discovery of a natural plant. Yes, it does. But this natural plant has to be discovered in a cultivated area. This means that there was an intention toward discovering that plant and that the discovery of the plant was not accidental. If it were accidental, a Patent would not be granted because it just doesn't belong to the person who discovered it. In this case, what the law recognizes is intention towards discovery.

It is even more likely that this plant is artificial. This is easier because it makes for more believability, backed up by intention. However, as mentioned before, a Plant Patent cannot be granted just because of discovery or invention, even if it is artificial. Here are a few conditions that bind Plant Patenting:

- The plant must be unique, and this must not be based on how fertile it is in the soil. Like every other patent, the invention has to be a non-obvious one
- The plant must have the feature of being asexually reproducible. In this case, the plant can generate more of itself without the association of any other plant

- There must be genetic identification with the original part of the plant during its reproduction
- The methods involved during the plant reproduction must be Grafting, budding, division, bulbs, and root cutting.
- The inventor must provide clear details of the botanical description of the plant to the USPTO or its equivalent in other countries in the world
- If more than one person did the invention of the plant, the other people involved or who contributed immensely must be recognized as co-inventors
- Plants like Tubers are not eligible for patenting no matter the reproduction they go through

Asides from these requirements, it is imperative that the investor gets both design and utility patents for the plant. If a unique and useful plant is invented or discovered, such plant must be protected both in value and in design. The reason for this is not far-fetched. For plant patents, the patent application goes public sooner than all other patents. This may be as soon as eighteen months after the first patent filing date.

The major types of patents have been discussed above. In this discussion, it has been inferred, if not stated categorically, that it is possible to get more than one patent protection for an invention. It is possible to get all three patents for a single invention, for example, in the case of the last discussed patent- the Plant Patent. A Plant Patent is needed, and a Utility Patent and a Design patent. Logically, getting a plant patent is unnecessary for instances where there is no plant involved. However, it is always recommended that a Utility patent be gotten alongside a Design patent so that the invention's component, functionality, and look are duly protected and vice-versa.

MEETING THE DEADLINE FOR YOUR PATENT APPLICATION.

Your patent application's overwhelming requirements and processes can almost make you fall behind. But you don't want to make that mistake. Falling behind Patent applications can be so annoying because it's like you have to start the whole process again. The other delicate thing about Patent Applications is that their requirements are not static. For example, in Chapter Three, there are so many claims listed. The reason is that different products and processes are being patented every day, and each of these products and processes has its specifications. Therefore, their requirements may differ based on the specialty of the situation, which any textbook or internet guide cannot accurately predict.

If you hire an IP Lawyer, these steps should be convenient for you, and you will not miss the deadline for your patent application- all things being equal. However, if you do not hire an attorney, you do not want to miss your application deadline because there are extreme measures that may lead to the throwing out of such an application. But why are there deadlines when these applications are all documents and requirements?

Patent Prosecution Deadlines

You have probably not heard the phrase "Patent

prosecution" before. It is a process under patent application, and it involves proving that a proposed invention is worth being patented. Because of the vocabulary associated with the phrase, you might think the word "Prosecution" connotes court, but it does not. The process starts with you filing an application and receiving a Patent. After this, you must think your work is done since you have a patent. But, technically, you do not have the patent yet unless it is accepted. This is after it has been subject to rigorous assessment under the Patentability rules.

Here are a few steps to ensure you do not miss your patent prosecution deadlines:

- Patent Prosecution processes are delicate and usually require the expert knowledge of IP lawyers. If you cannot hire an attorney fully, you can make them your consultant when you do your patent prosecution. This will take a lot off your plate
- You have to be adequately updated about every process in Patent prosecution. This is an intentional act and should not be left to Patent officials by waiting for them to call you or follow up. In this case, there is nothing as doing too much.
- Lastly, Patent prosecution support companies can help you go through the patent prosecution phase for a small fee or a contractual agreement.

Speeding up your Patent Application

This depends on one factor- ensuring that all the boxes are ticked. Once you identify the requirements needed for your invention to get patented, you should stick to these requirements and make the documents ready. This hastens your application a lot. It is recommended that you seek advice from people who have gotten their patents by asking them what you should do to speed up your patent application. Even if you do not know anyone who has done patenting before, having all the required things to get your patent is enough.

Patent Publications

First, there is a huge difference between a patent and a patent publication. Before you are given a textbook definition, let's try something relatable. During the Patent Application process, you will have to make claims to support your invention. A Patent Publication is an unofficial claim you lay to an invention before getting a patent. In this case, this publication is public, and it alerts everyone about what you are working on.
This unofficial claim is a publication of your patent application to the public. However, there have been some giving and misgivings against patent publications. So, objectively, let's examine them.

Advantages of Patent Publications

Publishing your patent application reduces the possibility of infringement on your patent before and after it gets approved. For example, if Marvel Studio announced that they were making a superhero movie named "Cat Monsters" and published this announcement. This is like publishing a patent application. Not only does everyone know about it, they know Marvel Studios is making it. Fox Century Studio cannot then say they are making a movie titled "Cat Monsters" with the same title and the same storyline.
Also, a Patent Publication can be a way of informing the public about an invention even if the patent application does not get granted eventually.

Disadvantages of Patent Publication

One strong inarguable point made in favor of discrediting patent publication is that it keeps competitors away. If you announce your invention to the world the next minute, a company is looking for ways to improve what you are just working on to become irrelevant a few years after it gets patented. At that time, their improved invention would then become relevant.

Takeaways from this chapter:

- Patents types are Utility Patents, Design Patents, and Plants Patents
- Plants Patents have more technicalities because of the specifications that accompany their reproduction
- It is recommended that inventors apply for both Utility and Design patents to ensure full protection of their invention
- Hiring an IP Lawyer or a Patent prosecution support company would go a long way in helping you meet your Patent Application deadlines
- Patent Publication can serve to prevent infringements on your inventions and can still draw competitors to you.

CHAPTER 5
How to Overcome the Patent Examiner

Of course, many people underestimate the role of a Patent Examiner when it comes to Patent Applications. After all, they safely think the person is a civil servant and poses no threat whatsoever towards getting their Patent application—unfortunately, many people who make this assumption find out that this was their biggest mistake.

Patent Examiners usually have a background in Science and or Engineering. Also, they are always skilled in all the processes involved in Patent Applications. But that is not exactly the important thing here. They must have the authority to grant or reject Patent Applications. In addition, they can review these applications and determine if the invention in question meets the prior art standards. Prior art refers to guidelines that set standards for whether or not an invention meets the requirements to be patented (Novelty, inventiveness, etc.)

Based on these reasons, you do not want to get on the wrong side of your examiner or do things that will necessitate the rejection of your patent application. This is why this chapter has been set apart to highlight ways you can overcome the Patent Examiner.

Meeting Your Examiner

The process of Patenting is a delicate one, and that is why different examiners are assigned to different Patent applications. First, you will have an examiner scrutinizing your invention to ensure that it is patentable. Now, you notice that the keyword here is "Scrutiny," which means to critically examine- that is the patent examiner's job, and that is what you will bank on.

When meeting your Patent examiner, the first thing you should avoid is that you don't want to come off as overconfident. Don't get it wrong. It is okay to be confident about an invention. But overconfidence speaks volumes that you believe that your invention is so great that there is no way it would not be patented. But the shock comes when the patent examiner can show you ten ways that your "super amazing" invention falls short of the patentability guidelines.

Hence, you want to become confident, ready to listen, and ready to adhere. It is annoying when inventors prove that they "know all" during the process of a patent application. This may spur the patent examiner to put your invention under unnecessary scrutiny. You need to comply with them with an unspoken recognition that they are good at their job and have the power to grant your patent.

Meanwhile, this does not mean you should come off as desperate or that your life depends on the patent application. Even if your life does, don't show this in an obvious way. It may give signs that you are probably hiding something, and your emotions are a way of covering them up. When you meet your examiner, be yourself and be ready to comply with their instructions.

Second, when meeting your examiner, you should come off as being professional and committed. The word committed here may also be synonymous with "serious." Showing that you are professional and committed will speak many things to your examiner and prove that you are willing to be dedicated no matter what it takes. As a result, the Patent Examiner sees that you are ready to make their work easier. Also, this is accompanied by having all the necessary documents for your patent application.

When you do all these, all things being equal, your Patent Examiner will be nothing but satisfied and worked on granting your patent application.

Foreign Licenses

Unfortunately, the rights to a patent granted by the United States (USPTO) do not affect other countries. Most patents do not have legal recognition in countries other than their own. After this, the only thing to do is to apply for a patent in other foreign countries. At least in the countries you want your invention to have a market. To do this, you will have to deal with a Patent examiner; and this may even be riskier because it is not your country.

Advisably, get an IP Lawyer in that country. You could even hire an IP firm that deals with helping clients get their patent applications granted. This is the best option. However, doing it alone may mean that you do not know all the things required to make the patent examiner's job easy and that you satisfy all the requirements needed for your patent applications. The requirements for patent applications differ from country to country, and an IP Lawyer or firm will help you scale through with your patent examiner.

For those who believe that granting patent applications should not be influenced by the inventor's attitude, it is important to note that Patent Examiners are human and sometimes may react based on their emotions. However, even if this were not to be the case, patent examiners have the power to make an invention come to life or never make it out of a notebook. This is why tips have been given to overcome them.

Takeaways from this chapter

- Patent examiners have the power to grant or reject patent applications. This is why they should be adhered to thoroughly by showing dedication to the patenting process and following up.
- Patent Applications have to be done in foreign countries too, and it is logical to hire an IP Lawyer

or an IP firm in the country the inventor wishes to market their invention.

CHAPTER 6

How to Overcome Rejection in a Patent Application

Yearly, the estimation is that over 90% of Utility Patents will get rejected. This does not mean other types of patents do not get rejected too, but the probability of their rejection is relatively lower than that of Utility Patents. For example, design Patents will most likely not be rejected as long as the design is unique. Plant patents may not also be rejected often because there are not many plant patent applications, and the ones there easily fulfill the requirements for getting a Plant Patent. So then, the question becomes: "Why Utility Patents?"
According to the US Patent Statistics Chart Calendar, in 2020, there were 597175 Patent applications. One thousand one hundred seventy-one of them were for plant patents, and 47,838 were for Design Patents. This means that over Five-hundred and forty-eight (548,000) of these applications were Utility Patent applications. Utility Applications are common because not only are they the most powerful, they are the model of patents, and every inventor applies for them. Therefore, there is a higher chance that those applying for both design and plant patents also applied for utility patents. However, the report further states that only 352049 utility patent applications were granted, and almost two-hundred thousand (200,000) utility applications were denied.

Apart from the fact that they are common, most Utility Patent applications get rejected because they have indefinite claims. According to Title 35, U.S.C 112 (b). Patent applications should have one or more claims that establish their definiteness and the distinctness of the subject matter of the invention. If there are not many claims in a Utility Patent Application, such application would be termed indefinite, and it could be rejected. Unlike most patent applications, utility patents require more claims because of the delicateness and nature of the invention. If the meaning of words that describe an invention is unclear, such a patent application would be denied.

Overcoming Utility Rejection

It is possible to overcome utility rejections. In the same report by the US Patent Statistics Chart Calendar, in 2020, five hundred and seventy-six of the two-hundred-thousand (200,000) patent applications were rejected, and five hundred and seventy-six of them were re-issued. The percentage is small, but it only means there is still a chance to overcome the rejection of your patent. Here is how to overcome Utility patent rejections.

HOW TO OVERCOME A REJECTION FOR INDEFINITENESS

When you say something to someone, and they don't understand it, the best way to make them understand is if you reiterate what you have said in clearer words. That way, you have amended the communication. This is exactly how it is with overcoming a rejection for Indefiniteness. As previously stated, this rejection comes from unclear claims made for an invention. Hence, to overcome the rejection for Indefiniteness, amend the claims made on your patent invention by making it more distinct and detailed. This will remove any ambiguity whatsoever. Once you can make the claims distinct, your Utility patent application will be granted as long as that is the only fault the patent examiner has with it.

LEARNING HOW TO APPEAL

Appealing the rejection of a patent application is as normal as it is common. Sometimes, the things patent applications get rejected for can be resolved. However, at other times, some inventors cannot seem to understand why their patent application keeps getting rejected. The resolve for these investors is to file an appeal. However, before you can file for an appeal, your patent application has been rejected twice. The reason for this is that the first rejection allows you to make amends to your claims, while the second one is an indication that your patent application may never be considered or granted.

Usually, this appeal is done to the Patent Trial and Appeal Board. The aim is to evaluate or reexamine the grounds on which the patent examiner has rejected the patent application. Your notice of appeal will only be granted when you pay the required fees for the appeal.

To file a notice of appeal, a form AIA/31 will be generated, which you will fill. Here are the things present in a patent appeal form:

- The patent of the invention you are reapplying for
- Your Application number
- Your Signature
- The Name of your patent examiner
- The fee to be paid for the appeal
- A Privacy Act Statement

HOW TO PROVE YOUR INVENTION IS PATENTABLE

To prove that your invention is patentable, you need to show and meet the requirements for a patentable invention. These requirements are Novelty, Usefulness, Non-obviousness, and Inventiveness. There is no way your invention will be patented if it doesn't meet these requirements. This is why you need to be a hundred percent sure that your invention meets all criteria.

Apart from this, make sure you explore all the claims possible to ensure the protection of your invention and the distinct explanation of its composition and functionality. Also, no invention would be considered patenting unless it is the machine/ device, a composition, or a process.

These requirements are the only way to prove that your invention is patentable.

How to revive an Old Patent Application

In most cases, reviving an old patent application is done because the application has been abandoned. This may be because the maintenance fees for the patent application process were not paid or because the inventor missed the deadline, in other words. Therefore, reviving an old application means that the application has been abandoned. Therefore, this process requires following the process for an abandoned patent application.

However, before you attempt to revive an old application, you must note the reasons it was abandoned in the first place. Then, you have to find ways of correcting these reasons so reviving it does not become a futile effort.

To revive an old application, you must file a petition for revival. Afterward, you are to pay a revival fee and correct the issues that led to the abandonment of your patent application.

It is recommended that you file for an Old Patent application revival within two years of the patent application abandonment. It is better if the length of time is not up to this. The shorter the span between the abandonment and the petition for revival, the higher the chance of getting the patent application revived and approved.

Requesting an examination Rerun

To understand what an examination rerun is, you first need to understand the concept of a reexamination during patenting. Usually, after the patent is granted for an invention, there is a reexamination of the validity of this patent by a third party or the owner of the patent themselves. However, this process is not compulsory; it is only done if a reexamination is filed.

If an examination is done and a patent is not granted, then an investor can request an examination rerun to ascertain the patentability of their invention.

Takeaways from this chapter

- You must be a hundred percent sure that your invention is patentable. This is when it fulfills the standard of patentability guidelines.
- To ensure that you don't face patent rejection, it is important that you are distinct about your claims and that you use the necessary claims to protect your invention and spell out its composition and functionality.
- It is recommended that you hire an IP Attorney so that your chances of facing patentee rejection are low.

- You should file for a patent appeal within six to two years of your patent application abandonment.

CHAPTER 7
Infringement and Violations

The greatest threat Intellectual Property faces is infringement and violations. Imagine going through the enormous stress of getting a patent approval or applying for Copyright and Trademark. Then after your Intellectual Property rights are granted, someone decides to start profiting off your sweat and intellect. There is just no logic to it. And the truth is that unemployment and bad economic situations are no justification for IP infringement and violations. Regardless of the wealth status of the inventor (in the case that the person has financial stability), thinking that a "little" replication of their work to get some money will certainly not hurt them is illegal.

It doesn't matter if the invention or intellectual property in question is a scarce commodity or cannot be easily assessable to people. That is the choice of the owner of such property. One of the biggest claims made by IP Violators is that it enhances the popularity of the intellectual property in question. For example, in Nigeria, the music industry is hindered by the illegal activities of music download blogs. The case made by these blogs is that they are trying to make music free for the public's consumption and make it assessable to anyone with a mobile phone. Even in developed countries like the US, the highest-grossing movies are leaked and uploaded on illegal streaming and download platforms while still showing in theatres!

The claim made by such violators is wrong in two ways. First, IPs like movies and music are made available to the public on legal streaming services and theatres. There is a reason for that. The owner of these IPs sign contracts with different companies and license the songs to them. It would be an outright violation to acquire these properties illegally and then put them on websites for others to download. Second, it is entirely evident that IP violators do so for money. Websites that promote illegal downloads get hundreds and millions of traffic, which generates a lot of money for them. So no, the least favored people are IP owners.

HOW TO CATCH VIOLATORS

There is always a way around it. You can greatly reduce the violation or infringement your IP is subjected to. If you don't do this, you risk losing a lot of income. This is because more than one website or violators infringe on your IP. That is underestimating it. There are at least a thousand websites that promote free music and movies. However, the case is that the higher the prominence or dependence of an invention on the internet, the higher its chance of getting infringed. For example, if an invention such as the IV machine were to be pirated, the circulation of these machines would be easily traceable, and the number of parody machines would not be many.

Conduct an Extensive Search

If you own IPs like music, movies, or books, then your main platform of search should be the internet. This should not be hard at all. As long as you go on a search engine and enter the keywords "download..." with the name of your music or movie, you will see several results of websites that illegally have your IP.

To address this, you can make an official announcement by listing the names of these websites and telling them to take down your IP. The failure to do this would then require legal action.

However, if you do not own IPs like movies or music, your research will involve physical activity, and you might want to hire people to this effect. You can even put these people undercover in target markets to see brands or companies infringing on your IP.

Send a DMCA Takedown Notice

Sometimes, when you search for something on search engines, there are a few words written at the end of the search results that complaints have been received, and that has necessitated the removal of some pages from the internet. This is referred to as the Digital Millennium Copyright Act, which protects Digital IP on digital platforms. Filing a DMCA complaint is very easy, and your complaint will be heard and adhered to almost instantaneously.

Punishment for IP Infringement and Violations

If, after sending a "Cease and desist" notice, the websites or violators in question do not stop infringing on your IP. You have no choice but to take the matter to court. You do not even have to spend exorbitant legal fees because the law backs you up one hundred percent, and the case is even won before it begins. The United States Department of Justice, in their Computer Crime and Intellectual Property Section, on October 1, 2018, established that anyone found guilty of counterfeiting trademarks would be sentenced to up to ten (10) years in prison and a $2 Million fine.

Violators guilty of counterfeit labeling can be punished with up to five (5) years in prison and a fine of $250,000. While for those that produce counterfeit copyright, they can spend up to two years in prison and a fine of $250,000. The punishment for these crimes may even be greater if the violators are making money off the IP of others.

Avoiding Naming Blunders

When naming your invention, brand, or product, you have to be careful so you don't name it wrongly or give it a name that is in existence. This is usually common for those who create things that cannot be patented. You can start a business and not necessarily apply for a trademark or copyright because the law automatically grants you the right to it. However, you want to ensure that you don't make any naming blunders or have similarities of name brands with other brands. It could create a bit of confusion when applying for a copyright or trademark. Apart from this, a brand that already uses that name can sue for copyright infringement.

Takeaways from this chapter

l Creators should ensure that their intellectual property is not subject to infringement or violations. They can use the right channels to shut down signs of violations.

l It is important to conduct appropriate research before naming your brand so you are not accused of infringing on someone else's IP

CHAPTER 8

How to Start a Business to Market your Invention

The truth is, getting a Patent for your invention is not the end of the process. It is only the beginning of the future of your invention. Realistically, you don't automatically assume that your amazing invention will get automatic financial backing from people because it is so novel and has a promising future. You may not be wrong. But the probability of automatic financial banking is very low. This is why you need to ensure that you start a business to market your invention.

In the US, patents expire after twenty years, after which they become public. This means you have twenty years to mine gold out of your patent. You want to make sure that you make the most of these years and get your footing right. This is why the first chapter of this book encouraged you to get your financials right from the invention process. Understandably, your invention might not get the needed financial backing during its making because investors sometimes do not want to invest in something that is not done or hasn't been tested or received public approval.

Starting a business to market your invention is not the problem, but ensuring that the business markets the invention is the problem. Unfortunately, so many businesses crash at their early stages because of several factors. This is why you need to make the best possible decisions while starting the business so that your invention gets enough profit returns to create massive generational wealth for you at the end of the day.

The question hanging in your mind is if you must start a business to market your invention. It is not compulsory, but it is highly recommended. And by highly recommended, necessary is implied. Here is why. Marketing an invention means that you are saying that you are looking for financial backing for it. This will mean cash inflow. You need a management team for this. You need employees to help you manufacture more of your invention, and you need a team to make sure that everything is in place. You do not necessarily have to run the business. You can be the CEO and appoint a Managing Director.

In other words, if you do not start a business, it would be more like investors are buying your invention off your hand, and you may even lose some amount of leverage when it comes to making decisions. You realize that you need a standby team to ensure that your invention stays relevant and readily available to the public. Besides, the more market exposure your invention gets, the bigger it becomes, and you realize that the invention is way bigger than you are at the moment. If you do not have a business or a company that manages the invention, things can get out of hand, and managing it becomes a problem. Yes, you will be shocked to know that sometimes, inventions fail not because of financial backing but because of a lack of business and market management.

With all that being said, here is how to start a business to market your invention.

Going Public

You have to admit that this is the digital age, and the best way to attract investors to you is to make your invention go viral. True, you might want to keep your invention a secret to keep competition away, but we all know that is not entirely possible. If you intend to share your invention with the world and profit from it, then the invention can't stay a secret. You may be worried about competitors, but the sheer truth is that even if they were to start working on a better invention to upstage yours, it would take years. There is no assurance that when they finally make the invention, it will upstage yours.

Therefore, you have to find a way to make your invention go viral. Drawing public awareness to an invention is extremely important. It makes investors seek you out. Think of it like this: There have been several scenarios where music artists were discovered on platforms like TikTok and Instagram. These music artists went on to get huge record label deals and now have prominent songs. It's no different from inventions. When your invention gets viral, you could even choose the people you want to invest in your invention.

Seeking out Investors

The saying is that "if the mountain does not come to Mohammed, Mohammed will go to the mountain." True, you have to seek out investors, but you need to be careful how you present yourself and your invention when it comes to financial backing. Any reasonable investor can see the quality of your invention and know how much they should invest in it. You have to make sure that you do not sell yourself short regarding investments.

The thing investors do is that they first undervalue your invention and then say that another invention will come up in two years to upstage it. This is a common occurrence, but that investor-act is already getting old. Facebook has been there for so many years, and it has not even been replaced by Instagram or Twitter, despite how cliché people say the platform is becoming. The important thing it has is relevance, and relevance is irreplaceable.

You need to establish to investors that your invention has come to stay because of its relevance, and that is why it cannot be replaced. Also, during this process, you should hire an attorney to help you close the deal and raise the bar for investors. Do not hire just any attorney that wants to get the job and receive their pay. Instead, hire an attorney who sees your invention's dream and is unwilling to collect fifty cents on the dollar.

At this point, you have to hold out a little. Most inventors do not understand that as long as their invention is as unique as they claim it is, it can make groundbreaking achievements. The fear of losing out on making money early on in the invention is why most inventors panic and sign investment deals with investors that will only put a lot of money in the pockets of the investors and crumbs in the hands of the inventor.

Hire a Team

This cannot be overemphasized. You need a team of people to tie up the ends of your business while you seek out investors and focus on your invention. This team will include your administration team and finance team. Also, there should be a team that helps you work on getting the best possible funding for your invention.

Formulate a Plan

You must have a plan to market your invention once you start a business. This should be done before you start a business for your invention because you can get caught up easily once your business gets on massively. If you do not have a plan, you might find yourself spiraling even if you have funding. You need to formulate a year-long plan to ensure that you are not stuck on what to do with it or how to manage the funding and expand your business when funding your invention.

It has been said that you need a business to market your invention, but you need to understand that the invention remains the face of your company. The name of the invention could even be the name of your business, which means the invention can be the business. The essence of starting a business to market your invention is for ease, administration, and public awareness. Investors and even the public will trust a business that owns more than a single individual with an invention. It doesn't sound fair, but that is how it works most times.

Key Takeaways from this chapter

- After getting Patent approval for an invention, starting a business to market it is of utmost importance. This is to enhance awareness and get funding.
- Inventors must be patient and get the best possible funding for their invention so they don't suffer financial losses, even if their invention goes massive.
- Hiring an attorney can go a long way in closing the best deals for investments.

Notes

TRADEMARKING FOR BRAND REGISTERED PRODUCTS FOR AMAZON AND PRIVATE LABELS

If you own a private brand, you could get a trademark and copyright. Even if it's a small business or you run it alone. As long as you created it, it doesn't matter the size of the private label. You are entitled to copyright and trademark rights.

Also, if you are a publisher on Amazon, you must have heard of Amazon Brand Registry. Amazon Brand Registry is more like a double-purpose program that gives you reporting tools on your products and also protects your products on Amazon from getting stolen, replicated, or hijacked. It would appear that this is the form of trademark for Amazon.

The reason for Amazon's Brand Registry is not far-fetched. A lot of people don't trademark the goods they sell on Amazon. Although they automatically own rights to it, the fact that they don't have any legal document that establishes that they own the products makes it susceptible to infringement. In addition, many people do not know that they can trademark their products on

Amazon. They can also own copyrights over the things they sell on Amazon. So yes, Trademarks and Copyrights are not limited to brands and companies alone. The products people sell on Amazon can be trademarked.

Although most people think filing for a trademark or copyright for the products they sell on Amazon is double work, it is all good for them because it protects their products from being infringed on. However, it would be better off if they registered for Amazon Brand Registry since it is Amazon's way of protecting its publishers. Therefore, it is recommended that even if you get a government-issued Trademark or copyright for your products on Amazon, you should also register for Amazon Brand Registry to get full protection and control of your products.

CONCLUSION

Practical Steps to Patent, Copyright, and Trademark for All, including Amazon and Private Label, was created for every person who can read extensively about Intellectual Property. Unfortunately, the subject of Intellectual Property has been left to IP lawyers and those who have understood its lingo for a long time. With this book, this is no longer the case. You don't need an attorney to explain how IP works to you. If you laid your hands on this book and took every idea and term presented in it in simple words, you could kiss ignorance on IP goodbye.

The first chapter did a clear exposition of what Intellectual Property is. This was embedded with relatable situations and examples to present Patent, Trademark, and Copyright in very simple terms while avoiding technical textbook definitions that may confuse the readers. The first chapter of this book made the readers realize the importance of Intellectual Property Protection. You can't read this book and still not see the importance of protecting your intellectual property.

In the same vein, Chapter Two expounds on how you should and can create your Copyright, Trademark, and Patent. This was done by showing readers how to file for their IP protection at the United States Patent and Trademark Office (USPTO) or its equivalent in other countries. Not only were the challenges of acquiring IP protection listed, the ways to overcome these challenges were described in realistic terms.

Understandably, there is the possibility of rejection during an IP protection application. This book tells you how to scale through these rejections and when to file for an appeal. It also emphasizes the importance of making distinct claims during patent applications.

Finally, it enlightens readers that even Amazon product sellers and owners of Private Labels have the right to acquire Intellectual Property Protection.

Printed in Great Britain
by Amazon

38596845R00036